Contents

Introduction

Just read it. Every word in this summarised document is true, and it contains the most important information to ever reach the internet. This document is written to empower the good people of the world against the tyranny which exists all around us in our world today. Effectively, the document presented here discloses concealed information regarding the extent to which medicine, science and technology has advanced in our **current** era. Moreover, the information disclosed here is presented **with the express intent** that it is made in the public interest and it meets all the criteria set out in section 43B (a-f) of the Public Interest Disclosure Act (PIDA) (UK) and the 'public interest test' -the Enterprise and Regulatory Reform Act (ERRA) 2013 section 17 (UK) which states that whistle blowing disclosures must be made in the public interest and should show one or more of the following-- [criminal offence, breach of legal obligation, etc]." Halliday (2013, p. 2). Furthermore, the Serious Crime Act 2015 (UK) section 41, 3ZA (which amends section 3A of the Computer Misuse Act 1990), states that it is a **serious crime**, punishable by imprisonment, a fine, or both, to cite hatred or spread hoaxes by use of a computer which would cause mass hysteria or public dissension.

From a legal perspective, the first questions the reader should ask are:

- If the Donald Marshall has been condemning public figures since 2011, why haven't any of these public figures issued a public statement against him, or filed a law suit against him?
- It is against the law to cite hatred or spread hoaxes by use of a computer, especially, that which will cause mass hysteria and public outcry; so why hasn't Donald Marshall been imprisoned, fined, or both?

The answers to these questions are very simple. It is because every word I have stated in my original letter since 2011 (Donald Marshall Proboards 2012), the full disclosure document (Marshall 2015), and this summarised document is true. Furthermore, the internet, and radio shows with small audiences, is the only form of communications which are not controlled. All forms of television networks, even including the Aboriginal People's Television Network (APTN), are controlled. Therefore a message as important as this, will never reach the average man or woman through television. Consequently, the only viable options are to spread the whistle blowing disclosures through communications such as the internet and small radio shows.

Furthermore, I am a victim of **current concealed** advances in medicine, science and technology described below. There are many, many, other victims of abuse, including myself; therefore, it is our plea: that you read this document with an open mind, and you investigate **ALL** statements which may initially irk you, and appear 'suspect' to begin with (the circumstantial evidence is available all around you); keep in mind that the abuse described occurs due to hidden advancements in science, medicine and technology; because as a victim of abuse, I can honestly say, there is nothing worse than experiencing abuse, and those who have the power to protect you from your abusers, ignore you.

Disclosure: Donald Marshall's Message to the World

My name is Donald Marshall. I have been cloned by a large secretive cult know as "The Freemasons" and "The Vril Society" and "Scientologists" together called the Illuminati. For readers unfamiliar with The Illuminati, see "The New World Order" (1990) by A. Ralph Epperson and Appendix B in this document; an introductory guide to the Illuminati and their agenda for the world is presented.

Furthermore, I have to tell you that human cloning, and consciousness transfer (which is the feat of moving from one body to the next) has been done since 1945. These facts have been confirmed and corroborated by other sources with insider information. The facts regarding human cloning and high scientific and technological accomplishments, are confirmed by George Green (Project Camelot 2008a; 2008b), Tila Tequila (Astral 7ight 2013i), and Phil Schneider (Schneider 1995; 1996; Open Minds 2011) and add credibility to my disclosures.

Key Figures

George Green

George Green (pictured) was affiliated with U.S. Presidential candidates, and was once asked to be the Finance Chairman for the next President of the United States. During his 2008 Interview with Project Camelot (2008a; 2008b), Green disclosed the following noteworthy information: U.S. scientists learned how to make people (clones) since 1938 -walking talking ones – and the scientists call these people "synthetics" or "the others".

Tila Tequila

Tila Tequila (pictured) is a television personality. In 2013 (Astral 7ight 2013i) she disclosed that there are cloning centres where human clones are grown; many missing children are taken to these cloning centres, and are forced to do depraved and ungodly things to each other by the ring leaders of the cloning centres. Tila Tequila is the first television personality to corroborate my original disclosure (Donald Marshall Proboards 2012) and my full disclosure on REM driven human cloning (Marshall 2015). See Appendix A which contains a link to Tila Tequila's disclosure, as well as, the transcript provided.

Phil Schneider

Phil Schneider (pictured) was a Geologist and Engineer who had 17 years experience working in government black projects carrying a level three security clearance. He is most notable for disclosing (Schneider 1995; 1996; Open Minds 2011):

- The 'black budget' expenditure of the United States; which Schneider claims to be between 1.023 trillion U.S. dollars every 2 years (over $500 billion per year);
- Deep Underground Military Bases (also known as D.U.M.Bs -"dumbs") and at the time of his lecture (Schneider, 1995) –that **there are 131 active Deep Underground Military Bases** present in the United States, and **1477 Deep Underground Military Bases worldwide**;
- Each D.U.M.B costs on average 17-19 billion U.S. dollars; paid for by the taxpayer; and it takes approximately a year-and-a-half to 2 years to build D.U.M.Bs with sophisticated methods.
- That military technology outstrips the general public's technology at a rate of 44 to 45 years of technology for every calendar year which passes. In other words, for every 12 months which passes, military technology will have advanced by 44 years than what we as the general public is currently accustomed to.

The implications of Phil Schneider's statements signify that since 1945 (when human cloning began), military (and concealed) technology has advanced at a rate of 3080 years compared to the technology the public is currently accustomed to (2015 – 1945 = 70 years; 70 multiplied by 44 = 3080). Furthermore, from the intelligence I have gathered over 30 years, each DUMB contains an entire floor solely dedicated to human cloning. Yes. Humans have been cloned since 1945, and continue to be cloned today; and current hidden technology in the year 2015 is as much as 3000 years ahead of the technology the public is currently accustomed to. I'll repeat myself: because it is **very important** the reader understands the above statement; even if, the rest of this disclosure is hard to fathom after first read.

The two **most important** things to keep in mind are:
1) Humans have been cloned for over 70 years (since 1945) and continue to be cloned;
2) **Present** hidden technology is more advanced, -as much as 3080 years more advanced- than what the public is currently accustomed to; and technology continues to advance at an incredible rate.

The Two Types of Cloning Techniques

There are two different types of cloning techniques. There is replication cloning and duplication cloning. Replication cloning is the type of cloning the public has generally heard of. Replication cloning involves taking the nucleus (the DNA) out of a donor egg, and replacing it with new DNA from the person to be cloned. After a few days the resulting embryo can be implanted for pregnancy. The newborn starts life off as a genetic copy of an original.

Duplication cloning, on the other hand, is the second **hidden** method and type of cloning, where the DNA from the person is grown in a big thick tank full of (salty) water. It involves a method of regenerative technology, where the cells are agitated and agitated, and over the course of 5 months, a fully formed duplicate clone body of an original is developed. The Illuminati used to have to use a tissue sample from the original or the cells from women's pap smears because this contained rich cells to make duplicate clones; they also used children's foreskins which were discarded at the hospital that got removed. That is what happened to me. I had my foreskin removed at age 4; -and by age 5, the Illuminati grew duplicate clones of me. Now the Illuminati say they have upgraded the technology since 2000, and now all they need is blood from the original. They then agitate the blood cells over and over again through regenerative technology, until a fully formed duplicate clone body of an original is produced. For readers who are unfamiliar with regenerative procedures, see Dr Stephen Badylak's video on "How to grow a new fingertip" (Science Channel 2014) and Carmichael (2013) which discuses how scientists cloned a mouse from a blood sample. Regenerative science and medicine (CBS 2008) does work; I have witnessed it firsthand, many times, in over 30 years.

Donald Marshall's Dilemma with "Mark 2" Sleep Driven REM Clones

The problem I am having is with Mark 2 REM driven clones. "Mark 2" is a rapid eye movement (REM) driven clone. In other words, Mark 2 clones are sleep driven clones. REM sleep is the fifth stage of sleep (Sleepdex 2015). The first REM cycle usually happens 90 minutes to 110 minutes **after** we fall asleep (Sleepdex 2015). What that means is: **currently,** this is the Illuminati's main form of communication. They do not call people on the phone; they do not meet at the Bohemian Grove anymore (they only meet there once a year for traditional purposes). Since they discovered the science of sleep driven cloning, they meet at the cloning centre **WHEN THEY GO TO SLEEP** (The cloning centre is a physical location, located 5 / 6 hours radius from the Robert Pickton Farm (Port Coquitlam, British Columbia, Canada) at a nature reserve).

Consciousness Transfer Happens When the Original Reaches REM Sleep

The Illuminati can transfer the consciousness of an original once the person reaches REM sleep if there is a duplicate clone of the original at the cloning centre, once the person goes to sleep (90 minutes to 110 minutes after falling asleep). Therefore, what happens is that the consciousness of the original is transferred to the duplicated clone body (the duplicated clone body is grown within 5 months by regenerative technology) once the original reaches REM sleep. The original's consciousness is transferred from the original's body; -although the original's body is still in their bed, asleep at home; -to a duplicated REM driven clone body at the cloning centre, and the original 'wakes up' as a cloned version of himself / herself at the cloning centre. It is a great marvel of science and one man's greatest achievements, but it is kept hidden and used for sinister purposes which I discuss below. I must address the readers at this point who are lost at the thought of duplication cloning, and consciousness transfer.

For readers who may have difficulty understanding the process of duplication cloning, see the video which features Dr Stephen Badylak (CBS 2008; Science Channel 2014). Badylak describes and illustrates how a new fingertip can be grown within 4 weeks, by the process of regenerative technology. Duplication cloning works a similar way; involving regenerative technology. where the cells are agitated and agitated, and over the course of 5 months a fully formed duplicate clone body of an original is grown. Moreover, readers should also view the Horizon documentary "Why Do We Dream?" (BBC Horizon 2009); the documentary clearly explains the phases of sleep; particularly REM sleep. The documentary also clearly explains that during REM phase sleep the whole body shuts down, and it is only the brain which is active. The fact that the brain is still active, although the body is inactive, is a perfect opportunity for consciousness transfer; and this is usually the moment the Illuminati transfer the consciousness of a person who is asleep, to a cloned version of himself / herself. The reader should also explore Petkova and Ehrsson (2008), and Ehrsson's (2013) lecture on consciousness transfer. In the video, Ehrsson (2013) clearly explains how through the first person visual perspective (seeing through the eyes), and through synchronous (occurring at the same time) stimulation of a body part, individuals can perceive and see the world from another body different from their original. In other words, so long as people can see through the eyes, and the body is stimulated, the match between the visual perspective and feeling body sensations allows the individual to see and perceive the world through another body **different** from their original. The consciousness has been transferred to another body.

Ehrsson (2013) also demonstrates that consciousness is linked. Once consciousness is transferred (from the original's body to the new body), even though the new body is not the persons original body, when the new body is attacked, because the person perceives the world through the new body, everything feels "very real". When the new body (for which the person's consciousness has been transferred to) is attacked, the original still perceives the threat as "real", and consequently, the person displays a biological and physiological fear response in their original body; the heart rate increases, as does respiration (breathing) rate, as well as anxiety.

Donald Marshall is an Original as he sits at Home Typing this Disclosure

This is how advanced technology is today. This is also exactly what happens to me. **I am an original as I sit at home here typing this disclosure,** but when I enter REM sleep, my entire original body shuts down, and only my brain is active. The Illuminati have linked my consciousness to a REM driven duplicate clone body of me. Therefore, as soon as I enter REM sleep, they are alerted to the fact that I have entered stage five of the sleep cycle, and in REM sleep, because they have a green and red light above duplicate clones at the cloning centre. The red light indicates that the original is awake, and the green light lets them know that original has entered REM phase sleep and it is time to transfer their consciousness to a duplicate clone version. They cannot transfer the consciousness of an original before REM phase or when the original is awake. When they try and transfer consciousness before an original is in REM phase it makes the original have intense headaches. Setting an alarm every 90 minutes to wake up and then go back to sleep also does not work in terms of avoiding REM sleep and having your consciousness transferred because the body requires REM sleep, and therefore you become very tired, quickly, if you do not get REM sleep. If you stay awake for four days without REM sleep you begin to hallucinate; after seven days without REM sleep you will die.

Do Not Panic, Riot, or Cause Chaos. This is Very Important.

Now I must preface this carefully, because members of the Illuminati have told me that I have to put this in an eloquent fashion, in a way which does not make people panic; because, people finding out about REM driven cloning, and the extent of the evil it has been used for, and continues to be used for; it could cause loss of social order, riots and anarchy in the streets. Moreover, I too **DO NOT** want riots and anarchy in the streets, despite the fact that I am vehemently angry considering the extent to which they plagiarised my talents over the years. If you are a good person reading this, and you want to help and you want social order restored for the benefit of mankind, promise yourself; me; all the innocent children they have affected through REM driven cloning, and the children of the future that you will **NOT** riot, and destroy a world for children who are going to inherit the world. **This is very important**. Remember the Illuminati have highly advanced technologies (kept hidden and secret), including weaponry, and they are just waiting for any excuse to use it on the populace. In all revolutions, the populace always win, and I want this disclosure and the end of REM driven, sleep cloning, to go smoothly. I want the good people of the world to keep spreading this information; keep spreading this disclosure all over social media, tell your close friends, your family, and as many people on social media platforms as you can. Remember, the internet, and radio shows with small audiences are the only forms of communication the Illuminati do not control.

Spread this Disclosure Document until it reaches the Armed Forces

I want this message to reach the armed forces, because currently people in the armed forces are following orders; yet they do not know how corrupt their governments and people in high profile places are. They are unknowingly defending these corrupt people. People in the armed forces will **NOT** defend these corrupt people nor will they harm civilians when they realise that these corrupt people have been growing duplicate clone bodies of civilians, transferring civilians consciousness to their duplicate clone versions when the victim reaches REM sleep, and torturing civilians in their sleep; having sex with under-aged REM driven cloned children; having sex with innocent and unsuspecting adults as REM driven sleep clones, against their will; torturing REM driven clones for sport; and for money-making ideas to benefit their own pockets while they make innocent civilians sick and have side effects in their original bodies from REM sleep driven cloning technology. No. The armed forces will not accept that. Therefore, keep spreading and sharing this information for everyone to see, so that it reaches personnel in the armed forces **ASAP!** I want the armed forces to overthrow these corrupt people. The Illuminati think they are very sly and untouchable because together they hold most of the wealth in the world. We must show them that they are not untouchable. Please do all you can, to share and spread this message. It is the most important message to ever reach the internet because **it affects all our liberties.**

I must also address the readers who may feel afraid in spreading my message because they may want to do the right thing, but they are terrified the Illuminati may degrade or end their lives. As unbelievable as the next thing I am going to share sounds, it is a belief system which shapes the reality of the Illuminati, and therefore they themselves, are afraid to do anything which may degrade their lives or 'eternal soul'.

They believe that they are the 'fornicators' mentioned in The Bible, and if they were to degrade or harm the lives of anyone aiding me, they would suffer the wrath of God when they die. Notice I said **when they die**. However, so long as they are still alive, they believe they can do all the evil they like, with little consequence; -as they do in their REM driven clone versions of themselves, at the cloning centre; worshipping Lucifer and doing all sorts of ungodly things.

They even say God does not exist, only science and technology; yet they are afraid of dying. Very afraid of dying; because they believe they'll meet God's judgement. I am just relaying what they have told me. They are weird like that. They also follow Hopi Indian Prophecy, Mayan Prophecy and Nostradamus Prophecy. They mix and match those three prophecies and come up with their own religion of what may or may not happen in the future.

How the Nostradamus Prophecies shapes the lives of the Illuminati

If you are left wondering why the Illuminati have not killed me, since 2011, when I started to disclose REM driven human cloning; the reason is because the Illuminati have said "If they do, everyone is going to know I am telling the truth"; -which I am with my right hand to God. I cannot lie about this; the things I have seen **firsthand** are too sinister and diabolical. It would make me as bad as them if I did. Furthermore, because they follow the Nostradamus prophecies religiously, they have told me they believe anyone helping me is considered part of "The Army of Light", and again, -to hurt or degrade anyone helping me, considered part of The Army of Light, would incur the wrath of God; and to hurt anyone considered part of The Army of Light will degrade their lives; they will suffer misfortune and entire ruin, as will their eternal soul. These are just some of the interpretations of the Nostradamus quatrains they have relayed to me. These people are beyond crazy, zealot and religious fanatics. Nevertheless, the main point to remember is: **you are safe**, and **they cannot hurt you**, **they are scared to hurt you**, as well as kill me because prophecies have shaped their lives and the lives of their ancestors for hundreds of years.

Furthermore, and practically, I have told too many people that this is the extent, to which technology has developed in our current day, and it is kept secret and hidden from the public for nefarious purposes and this is what the Illuminati do: REM sleep driven cloning. I have been spreading this information **since 2011** and not one of these high profile people, government officials or celebrity figures has issued a (public) statement against me or taken me to court over libel charges because I'm telling the truth; and their statements would not hold in court.

I have also told over a million Arabs; I have appeared on radio interviews with Vinny Eastwood (Vincent Eastwood 2013); Jeanice Barcelo (Jeanice Barcelo 2013); and Lisa Phillips on the Cry Freedom Radio show (Astral 7ight 2013a – 2013h). I have reached audiences as many as 280,000 views on the Vinny Eastwood Show (Vincent Eastwood 2013) alone. However, I must stress that YouTube reduces the view count of my interviews every so often in order to suppress the truth so that my interviews do not get featured on their platform. Nevertheless, **there is safety in numbers**, and rest assured there are new people waking up to the disclosure of REM driven, sleep cloning, every day; and therefore you can share and spread this information **without any worry** about facing reprisals from the Illuminati; even if you do not believe that it is in fact their beliefs in Nostradamus prophecies which is saving you and I from the Illuminati.

HIV/AIDS has been cured; so have many forms of cancer

Now is also a good time to share with the reader that this situation is not all 'doom and gloom.' In their quest to perfect technologies, science and medicine, the Illuminati discovered the cure for HIV/AIDS; cancer (except pancreatic cancer); Alzheimer's; Dementia and many more debilitating diseases which humanity suffers with. They relayed the fact that they found the cure for HIV/AIDS by stimulating the cells in an oxygenated rich environment because diseases/viruses cannot thrive in an oxygenated rich environment (in layman's terms). Magic Johnson was cured from AIDS this way and they use him as a spokesperson to sell the retrovirus pills which they know is not as effective.

However, the greed these people have, knows no bounds, and because they receive too many donations for HIV/AIDS as well as cancer donations, they do not announce they have cured HIV/AIDS or cancer publicly. As I've told you, and will continue to tell you: technology is far, far, FAR advanced than what you currently see around you. With the help of the good people of earth I promise to release these technologies for the benefit of mankind, and all reading this disclosure can hold me to this. You **must** hold me to this. It is time we ended corrupt governments and corrupt individuals in high positions of power in this world. Hold me to this.

I hope you are now beginning to understand why this is a **world emergency** and why these corrupt people must be ousted and overthrown. I also hope you understand why you must not riot or cause chaos because as I said at the beginning of this disclosure "I write this to empower good people of the world against the tyranny which exists all around us in our world today"; I **did NOT** write this to cause chaos, public dissension or anarchy. Good people of the world will inherit the earth once these corrupt people are overthrown. Therefore, under no circumstance must you destroy the world when you are going to inherit it. No matter how angry this disclosure makes you; no matter how angry the diabolical people who commit these crimes against humanity make you feel. Let's make sure this goes smoothly. Keep spreading and sharing this information, until this disclosure reaches the armed forces; until the armed forces bring these corrupt people to their knees. We are about to inherit the earth; by all means let's ensure everything goes smoothly. Now that you understand how important this disclosure is and that the overthrow of these corrupt individuals must progress smoothly, I'll continue.

Do NOT Be Afraid to Help. We Outnumber the Illuminati by 1,000,000:1

Don't be afraid to help. These people are easily defeated when good people stand together as one. These Illuminati people total no more than 10,000 people. 10,000 people against 7,000,000,000 (7 billion) people –that's less than 0.000001 % of the world's population. Now can you begin to understand how prevalent evil can be when a small organised group of individuals, as little as 10,000 of the world's most evil and tyrannical people all work together in unison to exert their influence over the world? The world does not have to be this way. We outnumber the Illuminati people by a 1,000,000 to 1. For every Illuminati person there is, there are **one million people** who are not Illuminati; therefore, do not to be afraid to help; all you will be doing is helping humanity rid itself of its sickness. So please feel free to share and spread my disclosure far and wide.

For those of you whom this applies to: remember the Illuminati (and I know it sounds ridiculous despite the evil they do) are deeply religious. They believe anyone aiding me is part of the "Army of Light" prophesised by Nostradamus; and to harm or degrade the life of anyone assisting me will bring them to their ultimate end and they will incur the wrath of God; they will suffer utter ruin and demise in their lives if they are to hurt you; they are very scared of people who can see through the lies and deceptions they have inflicted on the world. So please: stay calm; do not stress your heart; and know that **you are safe** and **they cannot hurt you**. You can feel safe in the knowledge that you can do the right thing by helping me. They told me this as REM driven clones on the night of 21st of February 2014 when I went to sleep. The above is exactly what they said.

For anyone interested in understanding the interpretations of the Nostradamus Prophecies, Crystal Links (2015) provides a good source for all 942 of the quatrains. Delores Cannon is also an author who has written three volumes called "Conversations with Nostradamus" and for anyone interested you can read these online (Galactic 2012a; Galactic 2012b) as well as watch her YouTube videos (CreativeForceVideo 2014; Disclose TruthTV 2015).

Yes. This is the state of the world today: a deception within a deception coated in reverse psychology; and fact is indeed stranger than fiction. Now after everything I have said, if you are still sceptical and 'in-between' on this issue; then the best thing for you to do is to pay attention to your dreams; or lack of dreams; –they are your own experiences and you cannot deny your experiences.

In other words, you may be having REM driven cloned experiences too; for some people they have a 'dream', where they are in the same environment, over and over and over again; or the theme being discussed in their 'dreams' is the same over and over and over again; or the environment their 'dreams' take place always appear to happen in the same 3 or 4 environments over and over again; –no matter what the theme is. In each scenario, there is a likely probability that these experiences are not just dreams; and in fact: -these people have had their consciousness transferred to their REM driven clone duplicate; and the Illuminati is trying to extract something from them; once that is done, they implant a false memory (see Kim (2013) and Alford (2015) for discussions on how false memories are implanted), which leads the person to wake up with the feeling of remembering something, but in actuality it is false; or you may wake up with no memory of dreams from the previous night's sleep; which means there is a high probability that you had your memories suppressed when your consciousness was transferred to your REM driven clone. This is why I say you can be sceptical about everything I have said (for now), but pay attention to your dreams, or lack of dreams; they are your own experiences, and you cannot deny your own experiences.

Noteworthy Frequently Asked Question

A Frequently Asked Question I receive, which is worth mentioning here, is as follows:
Q: Donald, if everything you have said is true...; in other words human clones walk among us now in a multilayered conspiracy which reaches the highest levels of government; armed with this knowledge what does one do exactly? What happens now, Donald? You obviously want to spread the word and make people aware but to what end?

DM: In short: I want to bring a complete end to the Illuminati and usher in a "Golden Age" of mankind. This question is best answered by detailing my 'Mission and Vision' for ending the Illuminati completely.

Donald Marshall's Mission and Vision on How to Bring Down The Illuminati

- This disclosure must spread, and **spread FAST and FAR!**
- If you now understand everything I have disclosed in this document as truth, then do not waste any more time. Share this disclosure with your wives, husbands, brothers, sisters' aunties, uncles, friends, co-workers, and children. We all have a part to play in saving the world from a premature doom.

- Call friends who have not heard from you in a while and tell them you have important news to share. Share this document. Share it on social media such as Facebook; Twitter; Instagram; Dropbox; Slideshare etc.
- Keep sharing this document until it comes to the attention of the Armed Forces. The Armed Forces will have to intervene. Once the Armed Forces intervene, we will have reached the middle stage of this vision and will be witnessing a complete end to the Illuminati. Until then, we're in the beginning stages, so please: spread this document faster and further. The quicker it is spread, the quicker the Illuminati are ended.
- Once the Armed Forces have intervened, a Military coup can be orchestrated against these vile people.
- Cloning centres can then be shut down once these people are overthrown.
- The freeing of any missing people (children; teens; adults) trapped in the cloning centres can commence (once the Armed forces intervene).
- HAARP (as well as other highly advanced technologies) can now be contained and not used for adverse effects against the world (once the world learns of this disclosure).
- These Illuminati people will then HAVE to appear in court for their crimes against humanity.
- Suing the Illuminati members in court (once court proceedings commence... we will be past the midpoint of my vision, and closer towards witnessing a complete end to the Illuminati).
- The populace (and it will be your choice) can then have their REM driven clone experiences restored and also sue and claim any legal reward / compensation.
- After the populace has sued the Illuminati for their crimes against humanity; the punishments can commence.
- Punishments will include: imprisonment and executions of these sick and malevolent people. The imprisonment and executions of evil Illuminati members will bring an end to the Illuminati.
- After the punishments and executions; Governments worldwide can now be replaced with incorrupt individuals, worldwide.
- The structure of Governance will also have to change. The reason for this because: future generations will always be able to check their leaders and governance more appropriately; so that the depraved and subhuman acts I describe can NEVER be committed against humanity again; nor will world leaders be capable of committing such monstrous crimes in such secrecy ever again.
- Ensuring that the laws of the land always progresses in line with advancements in medicine, science and technology; as well as, ensuring law progresses in the directions of Research and Development (R&D) regarding future technologies, science and medicine.
- Release of technologies, science and medicine which benefit mankind.
- Commence a "Golden Age" of mankind.

Empowerment by Virtue of Golden Truth

As you can see, despite all the horror of the world I currently present: if everything goes smoothly, the good people of this world, truly will inherit it. This is why despite any anger, sadness, or fears you may have: you must not riot, damage property or cause chaos or bring about any other form of public dissension. You cannot stay silent, or ignore the issue in the hope that the threat removes itself. You are called to act; you must take action to help bring the Illuminati to an end; you must act while at the same time, you must maintain your composure and resolve to ensure that the whole procedure goes smoothly, and we all inherit a world we want to live in. **This is of uttermost importance.** REM driven cloning is the most terrible thing in the world, especially when it involves unsuspecting civilians, and worst of all, innocent children. If you choose NOT to do anything, you allow the Illuminati to continue to clone your children, sisters, wives, and sons. You allow the Illuminati to continue to hijack the minds of your children, sisters, wives, and sons while they sleep, through concealed advancements in science and technology. You allow the Illuminati to transfer the consciousness of your children, sisters, wives and sons to their REM driven duplicate clone versions while they sleep, whereby the Illuminati molest your children, sisters, wives and sons, which will cause them to have learning disabilities, unexplained depression and suicidal thoughts, as well as, all kinds of side effects.

Your life, **at this very moment**, is more important than you may have probably ever imagined. You have purpose. Through you, and other good people around the world, together we can bring an end to such unspeakable forms of tyranny in this world. It is my humble stance that you have now become truly empowered with golden truth and you are now compelled to bring this tyranny to an end. If you have any unanswered questions, review the full disclosure document "Empowerment by Virtue of Golden Truth" (Marshall 2015) because it has been written to answer many questions concerning REM driven human cloning, and the current threat humanity faces. Moreover, the appendices, and bibliography in this summary disclosure, provide the reader with sources which corroborate REM driven human cloning. The glossary provides a list of key terms which relate to REM driven human cloning.

It also worthwhile to add that: I am **not** asking for donations. I do not want **ANY** donations. Ever! These disclosures are far more important than any donations. This is **NOT** my job. I have a job. I am an independent contractor; carpentry is my trade and I earn a living this way. If you sincerely want to help; the best way to help is to spread and share my disclosures. That is all I ever ask for, so that eventually, the world knows about REM driven human cloning, and the armed forces can bring these people to their knees. **That is all I want; spread, spread, and spread this disclosure.** I will **never ever** ask for donations. Ever! Please keep this in mind, and anyone who asks for donations in my name or on my behalf should not be trusted. I, Donald Marshall, will **NEVER EVER** ask for any donations. I hope that is well received.

Do not waste the knowledge you have obtained from this disclosure. It is my only hope to escape this man made living hell. It is my only hope, as well as the hope of many REM clones imprisoned there, as well as, real people who go missing daily, and are trapped in the cloning centres.

We sincerely beg you.

Donald Marshall

Appendix A: Thien Thanh Thi Nguyen (Tila Tequila) Transcript

Link: https://www.youtube.com/watch?v=7mRZ7ItF9ls&ab_channel=Astral7ight

00.00 – 1.10 min: You know what... since you f****** with my program darling Queen Elizabeth [II] and the paedophilia ring and the cloning centres, and the cloning centres. That's right darling the cloning centres. Parents listen to me right now, they are blocking me but that is quite alright. They are blocking me but that is quite alright. Because I have many, many, other forces; I shall not say their names right now, but I have many big plans to expose all of you disgusting, sadistic f***s! Okay? That is all. I shall save that for another time. But, however, I shall REPEAT: that was just an introduction to the reptilian family, leading all the way back. They call themselves the "The Black Nobility". Now that is just one part of it; alright?

1.11 - 2.47 min: The Black Nobility; the reptilian family; all the way back from ancient times; so which they think... they feel like they are the divine chosen ones... from whom may I ask? Definitely. Definitely not God. Our creator of the world. Reptilians: they feed on blood; children; the paedophilia ring; recently busted. Oh! It has been going on for centuries. Parents listen to me carefully. I don't care if I'm cutting out. I will continue this and I am not alone on this battle. Believe THAT! Believe THAT! I am not alone on this battle. I started out alone but I am marching on with MILLIONS; okay? So sit your old a** down okay. Because you are gonna roll over; but it doesn't matter anyway because you are all ancestral f***s! Who interbreed... ancestral f*****g... and then... and then... Oh! Only going to talk about cloning those children and... oh! And all those many children's parents listen to me carefully.

2.48 - 4.24 min: Hundreds of missing children come up every year. You wonder... why? How? How could this be? And then there is so called CPS [Child Protection Services] or whatever they are called; they come and take your children, just, just for nothing; right? Not to discredit everybody, because not everybody is bad. I'm talking about the bad people. And they take your kids... they take them as this... they treat them like... I can't even say the word. It's disgusting; it's sadistic. They... they... they take your kids... they toss them out like little [inaudible] cause they are so f*****g... Pardon my French, but then again when I'm dealing with these evil cum-buckets I have no holy words coming out of my mouth; because these are the only words they resonate to. So therefore that's how I refer to them. Because they can only [inaudible] ...their masters whiplash on them with these [inaudible] words of cursing, vileness and slaving and that is not what the true God is; okay? The God of Hell...; Anyways...

4.25 – 5.30 min: There are these CLONING CENTRES where they take your children and do sadistic things to them. I'm not even talking about child molestation here; not to mention; uh there is one of them that got caught, flying out to Florida; to meet up with a four year old little girl, to have sex with a four year old girl. That's right. Google it because it is so highly sinful... We have commercials about... you know starving kids; you know save the starving kids and it is heartbreaking. We can have commercials about it... why? Because it is a horrible thing and people can have commercials about it. WHY do we not have commercials about... 'Daddy please don't, don't. Mommy please don't let daddy let daddy touch me?' – because it is disgusting! It is so disgusting; beyond sin that no one, NO ONE, can even make a commercial about that because that's how sinful it is.

5.31 – 7.19 min: Do you understand that? Do you understand how sinful that is? These people, I'm not even going to call them people; alright? They take your children; they not only molest them; men f*** them and make them shoot each other. They give them guns. It's either you shoot him or I'm gonna shoot you. They are... mind you, they are children. Children. Yes. I'm speaking out, because I... uh! Who else is doing this? You're all just [inaudible]... shame on you... And actually the most recent paedophilia... got taken down... WOW, how long did that take?! Really?! Do you know how long this has been going on? *Sigh* Alright I'm gonna calm down... but as a parent and I love parents out there. My heart goes out to all the parents out there who have missing children. You know, we all pray for them; every day. And I put on a bold face in public every day; because there needs to be someone strong, believe that. But my strength comes from somewhere... that I have a very vulnerable emotional side where I feel very strongly for these children and innocent people. So therefore I want to speak out.

7.20 – 9.10 min: I have and I have my passion too; and in the end you shall all know why I am so passionate about exposing every single one of these scumbags; okay? The truth shall prevail and you all will know why. So as for you parents... ah... there are no words to describe. But let me just expose because you can't just... there is a point where you CANNOT just turn the other way. You know this stuff is going on; and you go 'Oh well... that's their problem. Let's just turn the other cheek.' How long are you going to turn the other cheek, until it happens to your own freaking children? When, when, when your own child; three years old, get's run out [kidnapped] and gets blasted right in the head with a gun... yeah... there's more to that people; okay? And I'm not just saying that coming from some... I mean, actually, mothers, fathers out there... If you found out... I'm sure you would do way worse than what I am just saying. I'm just using voc. I'm just annihilating them vocally. I'm sure the parents out there who find out what their children have gone through; their missing children. I am pretty positive more than just a vocal annihilation of these scumbags that do this to your children; okay?

9.11 – 10.32 min: So keep on turning the other cheek folks. Hey, go and turn the other cheek; you are with the others. I am not. I AM NOT. Like I said you... There is only two ways to go about this: you're either with us: the good guys, or you're with the others. There is no in-between. Cause if you are in-between, hiding like cowards, turning the other cheek; doing whatever; well then you are a freaking coward and you are just a sheep. And sheep end up dying because you know what you are owned by "The Others". So pick one: you're either one of us: the good guys or you're part of the others. That is simple as that! Two choices: good guys; bad guys. In-between you're dead because the bad guys are going to suck your soul out [transfer your consciousness to your REM driven clone] and do some sadistic stuff to you and watch, and make you watch while they [do] pretty sadistic stuff to your children as well.

10.33 – 11.33 min: Do you know why they love children? Because they are innocent souls; they're innocent... they're, they're the most innocent pure beings in this planet. They're not harmed by anything. They're new to the world; bright-eyed pure innocent children. That is why these disgusting paedophile and these clone rings; cloning centres; satanic rituals; Brownsville Texas... There are many other cloning centres where they take your children that go missing. And you wonder why? What happens to them? I'm sorry to break this to you but that is what happens. Now either do you want to know what happens to them or do you want to turn the other freaking cheek?

11.34 – 13.09 min: Tune into my next show. I'm gonna upload stuff; I have an arsenal ready to blow up! Okay. And I have reason behind this. You all should know my personal reason soon; but this has nothing to do with me right now. But know that I'm back, I'm back with a vengeance, and I'm back with an army full of people around the world who are sick and tired of treated like animals; or quote, unquote "COWS". We all know what that means. For the outside world (the masses) we all know the term "sheep", sheeple. But for the insiders we know what the cows are don't we? You know what "The Others" like to do with the cows, right? They start to herd you in... and to... yeah...I'm gonna end it at that. And to all the parents, families and children out there, I love you so much. I... have to maintain composure, because that is what I do. That is all. Over and out.

Appendix B: The Illuminati

Illuminati *–noun:* A modern-day criminal organisation operated by reprobate (depraved, unprincipled and wicked person) criminals. Their main agenda: is to enslave the whole world through advanced concealed technologies.

Today's Illuminati trace their roots back to Professor Adam Weishaupt who found the Illuminati on 1st May 1776. Since the inception of the Illuminati the intent has always been, and remains: "to bring about a NEW World Order that writes God out of the picture and deifies [glorifies] Lucifer." This intent is still prevalent today. The following excerpt is derived from A. Ralph Epperson (1990) *The New World Order:*

Weishaupt was a teacher of Cannon Law (law governing the affairs of a Christian Church, especially the law created or recognised by the Papal authority in the Roman Catholic Church) at the University of Ingolstadt in Bavaria, now part of Germany.

He even told the world, in his writings, where he would conceal the Order: "None is fitter than the three lower degrees of Free Masonry; the public is accustomed to it, expects little from it, and therefore takes little notice of it." He felt that this secrecy would lead him to success because he felt no one would be able to break into it. He wrote: "Our secret Association works in a way that nothing can withstand ...."

Weishaupt accepted the fact that all secret associations and secret orders had two doctrines, one concealed and reserved for the Masters... the other public ...." and the Illuminati was [and are to this day] a secret society with two doctrines.

Professor Weishaupt, its founder, boasted of his organization's secrecy. He realized that this secrecy would enable them to decide the fate of nations and because their deliberations were secret, no outsider could interfere. He wrote: "The great strength of our Order lies in its concealment; let it never appear in its own name, but always covered by another name, and another occupation." Weishaupt later wrote about that secrecy in a letter to a fellow member of the Illuminati: "Nothing can bring this about [the new world order] but hidden societies. Hidden schools of wisdom are the means which will one day free men from their bonds [the "bonds" of religion] Princes and nations shall vanish from the earth." So the secret societies were created to bring the world to the new society known as the New World Order. The members of these organizations obviously feel that their goals are so noble that they may perform whatever tasks are required of them to bring that goal to fruition. This means that murder, plunder, and lying all become acceptable as long as these methods assist its members in obtaining their goal.

Adam Weishaupt, the founder of the Illuminati, wrote over and over and over again, that "the ends justified the means." Weishaupt also told initiates to use whatever means, which included murder, to achieve the goals of the association that he was joining. And that the major goal of the Illuminati, was the destruction of all religion, including Christianity. That meant that if Christians physically stood in the way, they could be removed by simply murdering them. Weishaupt even went so far as to say that anyone not willing to take the life of another was unfit to join the Illuminati. He wrote the following in a letter to a fellow member in 1778: "No man is fit for our Order who is not ... ready to go to every length ...."

Another reason that Weishaupt felt that the Illuminati would succeed was the fact that he was offering his members worldwide power. He felt that this inducement would enable him to draw into his organization only those who would do anything to satisfy that desire for power. He wrote: "The true purpose of the Order was to rule the world. To achieve this it was necessary for the Order to destroy all religions, overthrow all governments and abolish private property."

But his religion had a different base than the traditional religion: his was based upon a worship of reason: "... then will Reason rule with unperceived sway." "... Reason will be the only code of Man. This is one of our greatest secrets." "When at last Reason becomes the religion of man, then will the problem be solved." Weishaupt's dedication of his organization to "reason" makes some sense when the reader recalls that "reason" has been defined as the "unbridled use of man's mind to solve man's problems without the involvement of God." The Bible calls this "the fruit of the tree of the knowledge of good and evil." It was this knowledge that God wanted man not to have, and it was the promise made to man by Lucifer that man could have it by eating of "the fruit." In addition, Weishaupt's religion offered its believers a reward not offered by any other religion: worldwide power!

Weishaupt wrote: "The pupils [members of the Illuminati] are convinced that the Order will rule the world. Every member therefore becomes a ruler." Weishaupt's religion not only offered power to his believers, but he offered them something else not guaranteed by any other religion: worldly success. He said that once a candidate had achieved the exalted degree of Illuminatus Minor, the fourth of the thirteen inside his Order, his superiors would: "assist him [the member] in bringing his talents into action, and [would] place him in situations most favourable for their exertion, so that he may be assured of success." Finally, the goal of the Illuminati was "man made perfect as a god - without God."

The ideology of "man made perfect as a god –without God" still remains to this day, and it is practiced by today's Illuminati members. The above phrase is what ties in Luciferian worship and trans-humanism. Lucifer is idolised by Illuminati members as the deity who gave man 'knowledge' and therefore is worthy of worship; God, -according to Luciferians, -did not want man to have knowledge and therefore is despised by Luciferians. Ingrained in the trans-humanism doctrine is the believe that: 'man can become 'god' through science and technology and in turn overthrow the Creator of the universe: God'. See LawOfIdentity (2014) and Mark Dice (2014) in the bibliography section.

These are the basics of Luciferianism. Therefore everything which is natural or pertains to nature must be contended or destroyed by Luciferians. This is why Illuminati members endorse having sex with children; killing first born sons; and drink blood. All the above go against nature and according to the 'edicts of Lucifer': paedophilia makes the person committing the act younger (it doesn't, it is just an excuse to act perverse on children because they know children are vulnerable); killing your first born son gives you good luck and fortune in this life (so yes, some Luciferians have sacrificed their first bon sons); and Illuminati members believe drinking blood / cannibalism is a 'purifying agent' (although in reality it causes spongiform encephalitis (holes in the brain)).

Modern-day Illuminati members still retain the goal of its founder "to bring about a NEW World Order that writes God out of the picture and deifies [glorifies] Lucifer." Infiltration through secrecy, still remains their mode of operation for the current Illuminati; therefore, they have secretly infiltrated all the major religions on earth; government and education – where each successive generation is being dumb down; they have continually diminished the ability for individuals to own private property, or claim inheritance; divided people against each other to continually diminish patriotism; and have continually diminished family values.

They also compartmentalise their knowledge between members. Until I fully exposed the Illuminati, many people who have been REM clones at the cloning centre did not know they were in fact REM driven clones, and thought they were in the 5th Dimension; the astral plane; a singularity; a spiritual realm; Valhalla; quantum hopping; a time stutter etc. or whatever else the Illuminati told them.

Today's Illuminati members also meet in secret -just like the founding members- but as REM driven clones, **when they go to sleep**. Furthermore, because Illuminati meetings are in secret and not many people know the exact location (because knowledge is compartmentalised) of the cloning centre; or the fact that their consciousness has been transferred to Mark 2 REM driven clone bodies at the cloning centre (and they are not in their original bodies); as well as the fact that unsuspecting civilians have their memories suppressed; the points mentioned above are the reasons the Illuminati believe 'they are all powerful and untouchable'; and as a consequence, today's Illuminati members do all the disgusting things they want; because they believe no outsider can interfere.

The ring leaders of the Illuminati today also believe "the ends justify the means". This is why they clone, torture, molest, murder, and rape unsuspecting civilians as REM driven clones in their sleep. The Illuminati of today offer their members incitements to go along with their agenda and not oppose them (or face death). Another popular method is to entice their target with many, many, wonderful prospects, and have the target believe they are joining a noble and prosperous venture, so that the target fulfils the objectives of the Illuminati unknowingly; promoting the Illuminati in a positive way, because the target has been deceived to perceive the nature of the Illuminati as 'positive'; by the time the target finds out the true intent of the Illuminati, and the evil which emanates from it, it is too late. Those who rise up in the ranks of the Illuminati are the men and women who have an insatiable lust for power, and most importantly: the men and women who want to rule the world.

Modern-day Illuminati members also wish to become gods (through technology); overthrow the Creator, and achieve their overall aim of enslaving mankind. This is why they clone people, and clone people in high rank society from all walks of life (movie stars, musicians, politicians etc.; whether the person willingly wants to be part of the Illuminati or not); so long as that person is in a position of power and influence, the Illuminati clone that person, and threaten that person, for example:- "Hey, you're going to hang with us –or else" –through such coercion, the people in high rank society who have power and influence will not oppose the Illuminati's plans to become gods; enslave mankind forever; and rule the world. Another reason for cloning high rank society is to include these people into the Illuminati (willingly or unwillingly) to ensure the world's populace remains in ignorance (because once all the world leaders and high rank society are cloned and under the coercion of the Illuminati nobody in a position of influence or power can warn the populace against the Illuminati) until the Illuminati's plan is completed and they have enslaved the world forever.

The Illuminati's overall aim of 'becoming gods' and ruling the world, as well as, mind controlling all the inhabitants of earth is also the reason the Illuminati:

- Administer drip feed disclosure through media; by telling some truths mixed with lies in order to conceal their true intentions and overall aim, and prevent the betrayed partner (the public) from ever discovering "the complete truth";
- Administer evaluative conditioning; by placing their symbols and ideology in popular media with positive associations; so that, the unknowing and unsuspecting public will eventually become predisposed to the Illuminati and unsuspectingly have a positive or neutral response towards the Illuminati;
- Because they want to become 'gods' is also the reason the Illuminati is promoting RFID microchips and only discussing RFID microchips positively, while at the same time placing suppression (gagging) orders on anyone who speaks negatively about RFID microchips; –which implies an unsuspecting public will willingly accept the microchip; and at the point of transaction, the person will have (unknowingly) given up their privacy to a third party (the Illuminati) for the rest of his / her life;
- Their aim to become 'gods' is also the reason the Illuminati are hurriedly trying to complete the HAARP grid across earth –because a complete HAARP grid will allow them to achieve their goal of mind control over the entire world; which fulfils their objective of becoming gods; because a completed HAARP grid will be capable of time travel, and therefore the Illuminati will be capable of going back to a previous time to correct the mistake(s) which led to their downfall; the Illuminati members will retain the knowledge of the previous time, and the rest of humanity will have no recollection of such a memory. Learn more about this in the Full Disclosure (Marshall 2015).

The Illuminati is **not** a joke. It is **not** fiction. They are very real, and part of humanity's reality; and through advanced concealed technologies the Illuminati aim to enslave humanity forever. The ring leaders of the present Illuminati includes Queen Elizabeth II, Prince Philip Duke of Edinburgh, Prince Charles of Wales and Vladimir Putin. I have detailed the actions of the ringleaders in the Full Disclosure Document (Marshall 2015), as well as, detailed other modern-day evil Illuminati members on my Facebook and Proboards (forum). It is time the good people of earth, stopped being afraid, do the right thing, put a stop to this evil, and save themselves, as well as their children's children from being slaves forever. Spread and share this disclosure.

Appendix C: Understanding Donald Marshall's Interviews for Newcomers

You can listen to the radio interviews I have done. Listen for consistency; particularly anything which you do not hear me, pronounce clearly for the first time. The best thing to do is to pause the recording at that particular point and replay it. You should also research the statement you do not understand. Sometimes reading helps comprehension a lot faster.

One of the main reasons you should pause and replay the recordings is because: the truth has been kept hidden for so long that a lot of what I discuss in my interviews are beyond most people's current world view; so at some points I may speak too fast for you; my audio/ microphone may not be so clear so you may miss what I say etc.

A friend has told me that when he first watched the Vinny Eastwood interview; he did not hear me say the word "scars" (When Vinny asked: 'How do I know I'm the real me?') although he replayed that particular point in the video 8 times. Everything was just beyond his current comprehension, at the time. No matter how many times he replayed that part he really could not hear me say the word "scars" –so he let that part go and played the rest of the interview, pausing, and replaying points which he did not understand, especially to comprehend whether I was talking about my original body or my REM driven clone duplicate body. He also listened to all my interviews for consistency, to note any 'slip ups', or any parts of my testimonies which do not 'add up'. He would listen to all my interviews, pausing and replaying parts he did not understand and he would reserve his judgements until he felt everything I was saying was for example as ordinary as: 'I woke up today, brushed my teeth, and took the dog for a walk'. He was also patient to realise the truth. After listening to my interviews he would just let it 'sink in'. A week later he would come back and listen to the same interviews, to test whether his comprehension on the topics I discuss has improved, and whether he can understand what I am saying without having to pause and repeat at certain points in my interview; and soon enough he could now hear me say "scars" at that particular point of the Vinny Eastwood interview. He had reached the point where all topics I discuss sounded to him like I'm saying everyday common place stuff that people have heard, such as: 'I woke up today, brushed my teeth, and took the dog for a walk'. For anyone who may struggle to understand the topics I discuss: I strongly recommend you take the above approach as my friend did; soon enough, you too will realise the real truth of the world like he has: REM driven cloning, kept secret and used for sinister purposes.

I cannot say the following is true for everybody, however, an unproductive venture a complete newcomer can do is to listen to my interviews first time, all the way through, without pausing or replaying parts which they do not fully understand; If you do this and if there is just a single part of my interviews which does not make sense to you; this will interfere with your understanding of the entire interview. Remember, all I am discussing is technology, thousands of years advanced compared to what you currently use; available today, hidden and secret. If things start to get too complex for you, reduce it to its bare minimums: (advanced) science and technology. I hope that helps.

Another thing which I do in my interviews, that friends have picked up on, is:- because REM driven cloning has been my reality for many years; I don't differentiate between my original body and my REM driven clone body. I just say: I did this, I did that, and (Queen) Elizabeth (II) did this and that, therefore it can become very confusing for newcomers. Please bare with me; although I'm more emotional as a REM driven clone, and not as smart as I am in my original body (this is a side effect of cloning: REM driven clones are more emotional than normal, and dumber than they are in their original bodies) I'm still "me" when my consciousness is transferred; I have all the experiences and knowledge which makes me, "me" and therefore I naturally do not differentiate between my REM driven clone version, and my original body as an outsider discussing these concepts would. I understand it helps comprehension so I have painstakingly done this throughout this disclosure.

I hope this helps; and I hope this helps to better understand my disclosure as well as the interviews which I have done. On the next page you can find the links to my interviews. You can copy and paste the links to your web browser or press Ctrl+Click – (hold "Ctrl" on your keyboard and left "Click" with your mouse, on the images below) to direct you to the interviews.

Vincent Eastwood

Copy and paste the link below to your web browser.

https://www.youtube.com/watch?v=M_1UiFeV5Jg&ab_channel=VincentEastwood

OR Press Ctrl+Click (on the image below) to follow the link.

Jeanice Barcelo

Copy and paste the link below to your web browser.

https://www.youtube.com/watch?v=3uzgu4ekT3c&ab_channel=JeaniceBarcelo

OR Press Ctrl+Click (on the image below) to follow the link.

Lisa Phillips (CFR)

Copy and paste the link below to your web browser.

https://www.youtube.com/watch?v=UonnFuHLJKc&ab_channel=Astral7ight

OR Press Ctrl+Click (on the image below) to follow the link.

Listen to parts 1 through 8.

Glossary

Aneurysm -*noun:* An excessive swelling of the wall of an artery at a fixed point in the body. A brain aneurysm is therefore a: bulge or ballooning in a blood vessel in the brain. It often looks like a berry hanging on a stem. A brain aneurysm can leak or rapture, causing bleeding into the brain.

Brain Aneurysm -*noun:* see Aneurysm.

Clone –*noun:* a cell, group of cells, an organism produced asexually from a single ancestor and is genetically identical to a single ancestor.

Concealed Technology -*noun:* hidden machinery and devices undisclosed and currently unavailable for public consumption. Concealed (or military) technology develops at a rate of 44 years for every 12 months which passes in comparison to the technology the public is currently accustomed to. Origin: Phil Schneider.

Cloning Centre –*noun:* a physical location (on earth) where duplicate and replicate clones are produced. These physical locations are usually Deep Underground Military Bases (DUMBs). DUMBs have an entire floor dedicated to cloning. It is also a place where Illuminati members meet with each other as REM driven clones. The above-ground cloning centre where many high profile people attend can be found within a radius of 5/6 hours drive from the Robert Pickton Farm Port Coquitlam, British Columbia, in Canada, somewhere at a remote nature reserve.

Cloning Technology -*noun:* the technological advancements in medicine, science and technology used to produce duplicate and replicate copies of originals.

Conditioned Response -*noun:* an automatic response established by training to an ordinarily neutral stimulus.

Conditioned Stimulus –*noun:* A previously neutral stimulus that, after repeated association with an unconditioned stimulus, elicits the response produced by the unconditioned stimulus itself.

Consciousness –*noun:* the state of being aware of and responsive to one's surroundings; a person's awareness or perception of something.

Consciousness Transfer -*noun or verb:* the process of transferring or copying the mental content (including long-term memory and "self") from a particular brain and copying it to a computational device; artificial body or avatar body such as that of a robot or clone version of the original. It is also the feat in which the person's mental content (long term memory and "self") moves from one body into another.

Depopulation *verb:* to remove or reduce the population of, as by destruction or force.

Drip Feed Disclosure *noun or verb:* is the process of supplying information but in small amounts overtime. Drip feed disclosure is also the process of revealing information slowly overtime, possibly telling lies to conceal certain aspects of the truth until the source administering the drip feed disclosure has adequate time to let out the truth in a slow and controlled way, thereby delaying the betrayed partner (in this disclosure, the public) from having the "complete truth" for some time.

DUMB *–noun:* [Deep Underground Military Base] a facility directly owned and operated by or for the military or one of its branches that shelters military equipment and personnel, and facilitates training and operations beneath the surface of the earth.

Duplicate Clone *-noun:* a fully formed human body which is a genetic copy of original developed through the process of regenerative technology. Duplicate clones are grown in a big thick tank full of (salty) water.

Duplication Cloning *-verb:* involves agitating the cells of on an original repetitively until a fully formed human body of the original is developed. Duplicate clones take an average of 5 months to form into a fully developed human body of the original through the process of regenerative medicine and technology.

Evaluative Conditioning *-noun:* is a change in liking, which occurs due to an association with a positive or negative stimulus.

H.A.A.R.P. Technology *–noun:* [High frequency Active Auroral Research Program] a radio transmitting system that can bounce signals off the Earth's upper atmosphere, (60km (37 miles) to 1000km (620 miles) high) back to probe deep into the earth or sea. HAARP is also capable of: disrupting human mental processes; knocking out all global communication systems; changing weather patterns over large areas; interfering with wildlife and migration patterns; hurting ecosystems; negatively affect human beings health, moods and mental states; and unnaturally 'boil' the earth's upper atmosphere. HAARP used correctly will control the weather without any adverse effects.

H.A.A.R.P. Grid *–noun:* a network of radio transmitters which can bounce signals off the earth's upper surface. Each transmitter is located at a specific point across earth and communicates in unison with other radio transmitters across the earth. At this present time of writing, a HAARP grid has **NOT** been completed, although the Illuminati are working twice as fast to complete a HAARP grid. The threat to humanity once a HAARP grid is completed includes: mind control over the entire world's inhabitants. A completed HAARP grid will also be capable of time travel, and therefore the Illuminati will always be able to go back to a pervious point in time to correct the mistake(s) which led to their downfall. Humanity will be slaves forever.

Habeas Corpus *-noun:* is [A] writ [formal document] requiring a person under arrest to be brought before a judge or into court, especially to secure the person's release unless lawful grounds are shown for their detention.

Heart Attack *-noun:* A sudden occurrence of a blockage of the flow of blood to the heart.

Human Clone *–noun:* The creation of a genetically identical copy of a human.

Ionosphere –*noun:* the layer of the earth's atmosphere which contains a high concentration of ions and free electrons and is able to reflect radio waves. It lies above the mesosphere and extends from about 60km (37 miles) to 1,000 km (620 miles) above the earth's surface.

Illuminati –*noun:* A modern-day criminal organisation operated by reprobate (depraved, unprincipled and wicked person) criminals. Their main agenda: is to enslave the whole world through advanced concealed technologies. See Appendix B for further discussion.

Mark 2 Clone –*noun:* Is a sleep driven clone; specifically, a REM sleep driven clone. A Mark 2 Clone is activated by transferring the consciousness of an original into a Mark 2 Clone **only when** the original reaches REM sleep (usually 90 to 110 minutes **after** the original falls asleep). Once the consciousness of the original is transferred from the original's body to the Mark 2 Clone, the Mark 2 clone is now capable of motion: such as walking, talking etc. The Mark 2 clone 'drops limp' and becomes motionless once the original wakes up from sleep. The original's consciousness no longer resides in the Mark 2 clone (once the original is awake) and therefore the Mark 2 clone is now incapable of motion. Mark 2 Clones are also known as "REM Driven Clones" and "REM Duplicate Clones".

Memory Suppression –*noun or verb:* is the selective removal of memories or associations with the mind using memory suppression technology.

Memory Suppression Technology –*noun:* any scientifically advanced technology used selectively to remove memories from the conscious mind.

Mind-Voice Technology –*noun:* an advanced technology capable of reading, listening, hearing and broadcasting a person's inner voice or thoughts. It is capable of replicating sounds **exactly**. Therefore an individual can hear the sound of drums, a guitar or any instrument and replicate that sound exactly just by thinking about it. Consequently, Mind-voice technology has the functionality of producing music.

Military Technology –*noun:* machinery and devices developed from scientific knowledge used by the armed forces which advance at a rate of 44 years for every 12 months which passes, compared to the technology the public is accustomed to. Origin: Phil Schneider

MK Ultra -*noun:* [Manufacturing Killers Utilizing Lethal Tradecraft Requiring Assassinations] the goal of mind control, using MK Ultra technology is to program an individual to carry out any task against their will and self-preservation instinct and to control the absolute behaviour and thought patterns of the individual. See Marshall (2015, pp. 33-34), and Appendix B of Marshall (2015, p. 87) for further details.

Neutral Stimulus –*noun:* is a stimulus which initially produces no specific response other than focusing attention. In classical conditioning, when used together with an unconditioned stimulus, the neutral stimulus becomes a conditioned stimulus.

Negative Association -*noun:* is an undesirable experience or perception.

Negative Stimulus -*noun:* a stimulus with undesirable consequences.

New World Order -*noun:* [NWO] Agenda. The whole NWO agenda is to turn humanity into mindless slaves forever; whereby the post humans / trans-humans mind control the entire world's populace either through RFID microchips or a completed HAARP grid. Another aspect of the NWO agenda is to depopulate the world's current population of 7.3 billion people to 500 million people (and never exceed a world population of 500 million people afterwards); ruled by a one world government; a one world ruler; with a one world religion. See Appendix B in this document for more details.

Original –*noun:* A person who is **not** a clone.

Pain Receptor -*noun:* Any one of the many nerve endings throughout the body that warn of harmful changes in the environment such as excessive pressure or temperature.

Positive Association -*noun:* is a desirable experience or perception.

Positive stimulus -*noun:* a stimulus with desirable consequences.

Posthumanism –*noun:* seeks to rewrite the very definition of being human. It is the condition in which humans and intelligent technology become intertwined. In the Posthuman there are no essential differences or absolute demarcations between bodily existence and computer stimulation, cybernetic mechanism and biological organism, robot technology and human goals.

Posthuman -*noun:* see Posthumanism.

Project MK Ultra -*noun:* see MK Ultra.

Regenerative Medicine -*noun:* (of a living organism) the process of re-growing new tissues after loss or damage.

Regenerative Technology -*noun:* any machinery or device developed from scientific knowledge which has the capability to re-grow new tissues after loss or damage.

REM Sleep –*noun:* [Rapid Eye Movement] is the fifth stage of sleep in the sleep cycle. It takes 90 to 110 minutes to reach REM sleep after we fall asleep. REM sleep is also known as the "period of paralysation". The involuntary muscles such as the brain become more active whereas voluntary muscles (those that you move by choice) such as your arms and legs become more relaxed or paralysed. REM sleep is a kind of sleep that occurs at intervals during sleep, and it is characterised by rapid eye movements.

REM Driven Clone -*noun:* [Rapid Eye Movement Driven Clone] a clone that can only become activated, once the original is in REM sleep. See Mark 2 Clone.

REM Duplicate Clone -*noun:* [Rapid Eye Movement Driven Clone] a clone developed by regenerative medicine and technology and is therefore an identical copy of an original. REM duplicate clones can only become activated when the original is in REM sleep. See Mark 2 Clone.

REM Driven Clone Death *–noun:* the process where an original dies because of constant torture to their REM driven clone or where a constant electrical current is applied to the REM driven clone resulting in death of an original usually in the form of an aneurysm or heart attack (because consciousness is linked) in the original's body.

REM Driven Clone Torture *—noun or verb:* the action or practice of inflicting serve pain on a REM driven clone. REM driven clone torture causes biological and physiological responses in the original's body because consciousness is linked. Intermittent REM driven clone torture (depending on what is done) causes the original to experience severe headaches, an upset stomach, achy limbs, sickness; a weakened heart. Continuous REM driven clone torture will lead to the death of the original; usually in the form of aneurysm or heart attack in the original's body.

Replication Cloning *–verb:* involves giving birth to a genetic identical of an original where the newborn starts life off as a baby and matures. The newborn is referred to as a clone.

RFID Technology *-noun:* [Radio Frequency Identification] are electronic microchips the size of a grain of sand that can be directly embedded into the human flesh. RFID microchips communicate wirelessly through the use of electromagnetic fields to transfer data. RFID microchips link the brains of people via the implanted microchip to satellites controlled by ground base super-computers. The dangers of RFID microchips to the implanted person are: total loss of privacy and total control of the person's physical body functions, mental and emotional thought processes, including the implanted person's subconscious or dreams –for the rest of that person's life! RFID microchips are also tracking devices, and the implanted person can be tracked anywhere on the globe.

Selling One's Soul *-verb:* to sell the use one's "Mark 2" REM driven clone to the Illuminati, for the Illuminati to use the individual's Mark 2 REM driven clone in whatever manner the Illuminati wishes. There are no returns once the individual has signed over his / her (soul) Mark 2 REM driven clone. When an individual sells their (soul) Mark 2 REM driven clone, the person has also entered into a contract to sell the Mark 2 REM driven clone(s) of their current children (if they have any) as well as any unborn children the person may have later in life. The person sells all their descendants (souls) Mark 2 REM driven clones to the Illuminati, once the individual sells their (soul) Mark 2 REM driven clone to the Illuminati. Selling one's (soul) Mark 2 REM driven clone is considered a serious business transaction to the Illuminati. There are no returns. If the person ever makes a fuss and wants their (soul) Mark 2 REM driven clone back, the Illuminati will either torture the person's Mark 2 Clone, or apply a constant electric current to the person's Mark 2 Clone until the person either has a heart attack or aneurysm in their original body. This is what public figures are hinting at when they say "They have sold their soul". They have sold the use of their Mark 2 REM driven clone to the Illuminati. Selling one's soul is not a joke. Never sell your soul.

Stimulus *–noun:* is something that causes a reaction, especially interest, excitement or energy. It is also an energy change registered by the senses. For example a stimulus can be a shinny object for a baby.

Technology *–noun:* machinery and devices developed from scientific knowledge.

Technological Advancement *–noun:* is incorporating, by means of experimental development, a characteristic or capability not previously existing or available in standard practice, into a new or existing process or product that enhances a product's performance. Novelty, uniqueness, or innovation alone does not indicate a technological advancement.

Transhumanism *–noun:* the belief or theory that the human race can evolve beyond its current physical and mental limitations, especially by means of science and technology.

Unconditioned Response *–noun:* is a response to a neutral stimulus we have no / little control over. It is a natural automatic response. For example, food is an unconditioned stimulus for a hungry animal, and salivation is the unconditioned response.

Unconditioned Stimulus *–noun:* A stimulus that elicits an unconditioned response.

References

Alford, J., (2015) *Scientist Implant False Memories Into Sleeping Mice* [Online] Available from: http://www.iflscience.com/brain/scientists-implant-false-memories-sleeping-mice [Accessed 28th July 2015]

Astral 7sight (2013a) *Illuminati Exposed 2013: Chemtrails, Atlantis, Clones, Drones & Vril Part 1/8.* [Online video]. June 23rd 2013. Available from: https://www.youtube.com/watch?v=UonnFuHLJKc&ab_channel=Astral7ight [Accessed 12th July 2015]

Astral 7sight (2013b) *Illuminati Exposed 2013: Chemtrails, Atlantis, Clones, Drones & Vril Part 2/8.* [Online video]. June 23rd 2013. Available from: https://www.youtube.com/watch?v=QPAXCwu5MIo&ab_channel=Astral7ight [Accessed 12th July 2015]

Astral 7sight (2013c) *Illuminati Exposed 2013: Chemtrails, Atlantis, Clones, Drones & Vril Part 3/8.* [Online video]. June 23rd 2013. Available from: https://www.youtube.com/watch?v=5zlJ0VQP444&ab_channel=Astral7ight [Accessed 12th July 2015]

Astral 7sight (2013d) *Illuminati Exposed 2013: Chemtrails, Atlantis, Clones, Drones & Vril Part 4/8.* [Online video]. June 23rd 2013. Available from: https://www.youtube.com/watch?v=dCGhrDEl-q8&ab_channel=Astral7ight [Accessed 12th July 2015]

Astral 7sight (2013e) *Illuminati Exposed 2013: Chemtrails, Atlantis, Clones, Drones & Vril Part 5/8.* [Online video]. June 23rd 2013. Available from: https://www.youtube.com/watch?v=EDyerA-k8Ic&ab_channel=Astral7ight [Accessed 12th July 2015]

Astral 7sight (2013f) *Illuminati Exposed 2013: Chemtrails, Atlantis, Clones, Drones & Vril Part 6/8.* [Online video]. June 23rd 2013. Available from: https://www.youtube.com/watch?v=iqQZPpXl2yg&ab_channel=Astral7ight [Accessed 12th July 2015]

Astral 7sight (2013g) *Illuminati Exposed 2013: Chemtrails, Atlantis, Clones, Drones & Vril Part 7/8.* [Online video]. June 23rd 2013. Available from: https://www.youtube.com/watch?v=WYZSOnyWwP8&ab_channel=Astral7ight [Accessed 12th July 2015]

Astral 7sight (2013h) *Illuminati Exposed 2013: Chemtrails, Atlantis, Clones, Drones & Vril Part 8/8.* [Online video]. June 23rd 2013. Available from: https://www.youtube.com/watch?v=Y18m0gPLQhM&ab_channel=Astral7ight [Accessed 12th July 2015]

Astral 7sight (2013i) *Celebrity Tila Tequila: Missing Children and Cloning Centers* [Online video]. June 7th 2013. Available from:
https://www.youtube.com/watch?v=7mRZ7ItF9ls&ab_channel=Astral7ight [Accessed 12th July 2015]

BBC Horizon (2009) *Why Do We Dream BBC Horizon* [Online video]. May 15th 2013. Available from:
https://www.youtube.com/watch?v=E8MZ1twv0cU&ab_channel=AHOlearning [Accessed: 7th June 2015]

Carmichael, J., (2013) *Mouse Cloned From A Mere Drop of Blood* [Online] Available from:
http://www.popsci.com/science/article/2013-06/mouse-cloned-mere-drop-blood [Accessed 19th July 2015]

CBS (2008) *Regeneration of Cells – Regrowing finger* [Online video] May 15th 2010. Available from:
https://www.youtube.com/watch?v=ITxx2sOLW2Y&ab_channel=Weltenspur2 [Accessed: 25th June 2015]

CreativeForceVideo (2014) *Speaking with Nostradamus, Quantum Hypnosis with Delores Cannon* [Online video] August 2nd 2014. Available from:
https://www.youtube.com/watch?v=CBOml6LTbpM&ab_channel=CreativeForceVideo [Accessed 25th July 2015]

Crystal Links (2015) *Nostradamus* [Online] Available from:
http://www.crystalinks.com/nostradamus.html [Accessed 25th July 2015]

Disclose TruthTV (2015) *Delores Cannon on WW3, Antichrist Nostradamus Prophecies [Full Video]* [Online video] March 19th 2015. Available from:
https://www.youtube.com/watch?v=l0aCHrY0ObI&ab_channel=DiscloseTruthTV [Accessed 26th July 2015]

Donald Marshall Proboards (2012) *DONALD'S ORIGINAL LETTER TO THE PUBLIC..* [Online] Available from: http://donaldmarshall.proboards.com/thread/75/donalds-original-letter-public [Accessed: 28th July 2015]

Ehrsson, H.H., (2013) *Inspirational Lecture –Professor Henrik Ehrsson* [Online video] October 3rd 2013. Available from:
https://www.youtube.com/watch?v=iR7HissYN2U&ab_channel=karolinskainstitutet [Accessed 2nd July 2013]

Epperson, A. R., (1990) *The New World Order*, Publius Press. [Online] Available from:
https://ia700406.us.archive.org/27/items/TheNewWorldOrder_342/TheNewWorldOrder.pdf [Accessed 7th July 2015]

Galactic (2012a) *Conversations With Nostradamus Volume One* [Online] Available from: http://galactic.no/rune/DoloresCannon_books/Dolores-Cannon-Conversations-With-Nostradamus-Volume-1.pdf [Accessed 25th July 2015]

Galactic (2012b) *Conversations With Nostradamus Volume Two* [Online] Available from: http://galactic.no/rune/DoloresCannon_books/Dolores-Cannon-Conversations-With-Nostradamus-V2.pdf [Accessed 25th July 2015]

Halliday, P., (2013) *Whistleblowing: the new 'public interest' test and other developments.* [Online] Available from: http://www.11kbw.com/uploads/files/PHPaper.pdf [Accessed 8th May 2015], p. 2

Jeanice Barcelo (2013) *BNE Radio Show w/ guest Donald Marshall* [Online video]. March 9th 2013. Available from: https://www.youtube.com/watch?v=3uzgu4ekT3c&ab_channel=JeaniceBarcelo [Accessed 11th July 2015]

Kim, M., (2013) *MIT scientists implant a false memory into a mouse's brain* [Online] Available from: http://www.washingtonpost.com/national/health-science/inception-mit-scientists-implant-a-false-memory-into-a-mouses-brain/2013/07/25/47bdee7a-f49a-11e2-a2f1-a7acf9bd5d3a_story.html [Accessed 28th July 2015]

Marshall, D., (2015) *Empowerment by Virtue of Golden Truth. Human Cloning: Specifically REM Driven Human Cloning. Full Disclosure.* Unpublished.

Open Minds (2011) *Phil Schneider's incredible ET claims.* [Online] Available from: http://www.openminds.tv/phil-schneiders-incredible-et-claims/9982 [Accessed 9th May 2015]

Petkova, V. I., and Ehrsson, H.H., (2008) *If I Were You: Perceptual Illusion of Body Swapping,* PLoS ONE, Volume 3, Issue 12, pp. 1-9

Project Camelot (2008a) *Project Camelot Interviews George Green – Part 1 of 2* [Online video]. April 16th 2008. Available from: https://www.youtube.com/watch?v=sSYXrWIA618&ab_channel=ProjectCamelot [Accessed: 11th May 2015]

Project Camelot (2008b) *Project Camelot Interviews George Green – Part 2 of 2* [Online video]. April 16th 2008. Available from: https://www.youtube.com/watch?v=6zSrg0IxHzI&ab_channel=ProjectCamelot [Accessed: 11th May 2015]

Schneider, P., (1995) *Phil Schneider Documentary of truth about Aliens & UFO's & our Government.* [Online video]. September 21st 2013. Available from: https://www.youtube.com/watch?v=Oljrjxnixtw&ab_channel=AliensAmongUs [Accessed: 10th May 2015]

Schneider, P., (1996) *Phil Schneider's Last Speech ~ Two Months Before His Assassination ~ Aliens & Underground Bases* [Online video]. November 24th 2013. Available from: https://www.youtube.com/watch?v=Slgb5U-OqFM&ab_channel=FallofMedia [Accessed: 10th May 2015]

Science Channel (2014) *How to Grow a New Fingertip | World's Strangest.* [Online video] June 16th 2014. Available from: https://www.youtube.com/watch?v=DtBUM51t4iw&ab_channel=ScienceChannel [Accessed 23rd June 2015]

Sleepdex (2015) *Stages of Sleep* [Online] Available from: http://www.sleepdex.org/stages.htm [Accessed: 5th June 2015]

Vincent Eastwood (2013) *Illuminati Cloning Programs, Sex and Murder Cults and Reptilians! 26Feb2013* [Online video] February 26th 2013. Available from: https://www.youtube.com/watch?v=M_1UiFeV5Jg&ab_channel=VincentEastwood [10th July 2015]

Bibliography

2045 Initiative (2015) *2045 Strategic Social Initiative* [Online] Available from: http://2045.com/ [Accessed 1st June 2015]

Albrecht, K., and McIntyre (2005) *Spychips: How Major Corporations and Government Plan to Track Your Every Move with RFID.* Plume

Alford, J., (2015) *Scientist Implant False Memories Into Sleeping Mice* [Online] Available from: http://www.iflscience.com/brain/scientists-implant-false-memories-sleeping-mice [Accessed 28th July 2015]

Animal Research (1996) *Cloning Dolly the Sheep* [Online] Available from: http://www.animalresearch.info/en/medical-advances/timeline/cloning-dolly-the-sheep/ [Accessed 28th June 2014]

Anthony, S., (2012) *GoFlow: a DIY tDCS brain-boosting kit* [Online] Available from: http://www.extremetech.com/extreme/121861-goflow-a-diy-tdcs-brain-boosting-kit [Accessed 24th May 2015]

Anthony, S., (2013) *What is transhumanism, or, what does it mean to be human?* [Online] Available from: http://www.extremetech.com/extreme/152240-what-is-transhumanism-or-what-does-it-mean-to-be-human [Accessed 24th May 2015]

Avatar (2009) Film. Directed by James Cameron. [DVD]. UK: 20th Century Fox

BBC Future (2015) *BBC Future* [Online] Available from: http://www.bbc.com/future [Accessed 28th July 2015]

BBC News (2000) *Scientist 'clone' monkey* [Online] Available from: http://news.bbc.co.uk/1/hi/sci/tech/602027.stm [Accessed: 28th June 2015]

BBC News (2015a) *BBC News* [Online] Available from: http://www.bbc.co.uk/news/science_and_environment [Accessed 28th July 2015]

BBC News (2015b) *BBC News* [Online] Available from: http://www.bbc.co.uk/news/technology [Accessed 28th July]

BEAMS (2007) *BT's 'Soul Catcher2025' Implants* [Online] Available from: http://www.beamsinvestigations.org/BT's%20'Soul%20Catcher%202025'%20Implants.htm [Accessed 1st June 2015]

Begich, N., & Manning, J., (1997) *ANGELS DON'T PLAY THIS HAARP. Advances in Tesla Technology* [Online] Available from: http://www.alachuacounty.us/Depts/epd/EPAC/Angels%20Dont%20Play%20This%20HAARP%20by%20Nick%20Begich%201997.pdf [Accessed 15th June 2015]

Berkeley News (2011) *Scientists use brain imaging to reveal the movies in our mind* [Online] Available from: http://news.berkeley.edu/2011/09/22/brain-movies/ [Accessed: 22nd July 2015]

Beter, P., (2011) *"Organic Robotoids are real" by Dr Peter Beter* [Online video]. April 15th 2011. Available from: https://www.youtube.com/watch?v=nc0m5UMPwtU&ab_channel=youlittlerocket [Accessed 6th July 2015]

Bloomberg Business (2015) *See Future of Artificial Intelligence in Mind Clones Right Now!* [Online video] Available from: https://www.youtube.com/watch?v=4bqZp9TPYVk&ab_channel=BloombergBusiness [Accessed 27th June 2015]

Borghino, D., (2012) *"Avatar" project aims for human immortality by 2045* [Online] Available from: http://www.gizmag.com/avatar-project-2045/23454/ [Accessed 3rd June 2015]

Boringest (2006) *Bush Video 10 years ago!* [Online video]. January 3rd 2006. Available from: https://www.youtube.com/watch?v=pw4Bhmm22xo&ab_channel=boringest [Accessed: 11th May 2015]

BritneySpearsVevo (2009) *Britney Spears –Break The Ice* [Online video] October 24th 2009. Available from: https://www.youtube.com/watch?v=eQFIKP9rGhQ&ab_channel=BritneySpearsVEVO [Accessed 18th July 2015]

BritneySpearsVevo (2011) *Britney Spears –Hold it Against me* [Online video] February 17th 2011. Available from: https://www.youtube.com/watch?v=-Edv8Onsrgg&ab_channel=BritneySpearsVEVO [Accessed 18th July 2015]

Campbell, T., (2008) *Physics, Metaphysics and the nature of Consciousness* [Dr Thomas Campbell –My Big TOE (1 of 18)] [Online video] May 25th 2008. Available from: https://www.youtube.com/watch?v=MxECb7zcQhQ&list=PLBFFCEB1CAEDF9E6C&ab_channel=akn0ledge [Accessed 4th July 2015]

Cherry, K., (2015) *What is Consciousness* [Online] Available from: http://psychology.about.com/od/statesofconsciousness/f/consciousness.htm [Accessed 1st July 2015]

CTForecaster (2013) *Japanese Dream Recording Machine –Update* [Online video]. April 12th 2013. Available from: https://www.youtube.com/watch?v=gQueU9a8URw&ab_channel=CTForecaster [Accessed: 22nd July 2015]

Daily Mail Online (2015) *Mail Online* [Online] Available from: http://www.dailymail.co.uk/sciencetech/index.html [Accessed 28th July 2015]

De Houwer, J., Thomas, S., & Baeyens, F. (2001) *Associative Learning of Likes and Dislikes: A Review of 25 years of Research on Human Evaluative Conditioning.* Psychological Bulletin, Vol. 127, No.6, 853-869 In Hale, J., (2012) *What influences are Food Likes and Dislikes?* [Online] Available from: http://psychcentral.com/blog/archives/2012/02/15/what-influences-our-food-likes-and-dislikes/ [Accessed 28th June 2015]

Dictionary Reference (2015) *Consciousness* [Online] Available from: http://dictionary.reference.com/browse/consciousness?s=t [Accessed 30th June 2015]

Donald Marshall Proboards (2015) *Donald Marshall Proboards* [Online] Available from: http://donaldmarshall.proboards.com/ [28th July 2015]

Fox 4 News –Dallas Fort Worth (2014) *Aug. 15, 1988 – George W. Bush –KDFW* [Online video]. June 23rd 2014. Available from: https://www.youtube.com/watch?v=zwrl2axvPmY&ab_channel=FOX4News-Dallas-FortWorth [Accessed: 15th May 2015]

FW: Thinking (2014) *Erase and Restore your memories* [Online video]. Jun 18th 2014. Available from: https://www.youtube.com/watch?v=PpzzD_103jc&ab_channel=FW:Thinking [Accessed 8th July 2015]

Gizmag (2015) *Gizmag* [Online] Available from: http://www.gizmag.com/ [Accessed 28th July 2015]

Greenberg, P., (2013) *No More Bad Flashback: Scientist Find Gene That Erases Memories* [Online] Available from: http://mashable.com/2013/09/25/erase-bad-memories/ [Accessed 11th June 2015]

Hale, J., (2012) *What influences are Food Likes and Dislikes?* [Online] Available from: http://psychcentral.com/blog/archives/2012/02/15/what-influences-our-food-likes-and-dislikes/ [Accessed 28th June 2015]

Hewitt, J., (2012) *How to create a mind or die trying* [Online] Available from: http://www.extremetech.com/extreme/141507-how-to-create-a-mind-or-die-trying [Accessed 24th May 2015]

History (2015) *George W. Bush* [Online] Available from: http://www.history.com/topics/us-presidents/george-w-bush [Accessed 14th May 2015]

Hostel (2006) Film. Directed by Eli Roth. [DVD]. USA: Lionsgate

Hostel: Part II (2007) Film. Directed by Eli Roth. [DVD]. USA: Lionsgate

Hostel: Part III (2011) Film. Directed by Scott Spiegel. [DVD]. USA: Sony Pictures Home Entertainment

Inception (2010) Film. Directed by Christopher Nolan. [DVD]. UK: Warner Bros. Pictures

inifiniLor (2013) *Appeal from Survivors of Canadian Genocide* [Online video]. April 8th 2013. Available from: https://www.youtube.com/watch?v=cVYkctM1k90&ab_channel=infiniLor [Accessed 13th July 2015]

Jim Cristea (2009) *Mind Reading - FMRI - Machine that Reads Your Thoughts - 60 Minutes* [Online video]. January 9th 2009. Available from: https://www.youtube.com/watch?v=Cwda7YWK0WQ&ab_channel=JimCristea [Accessed: 22nd July 2015]

Jones, A., (2008) *Reflections and Warnings: An Interview with Aaron Russo* [Online video]. June 1st 2009. Available from: https://www.youtube.com/watch?v=YGAaPjqdbgQ&ab_channel=rohstyles23 [Accessed: 12th May 2015]

KafkaWinstonWorld (2014) *IS THIS WHERE WE ARE GOING? THIS MOVIE WILL BLOW YOUR F%$NG MIND(mirrored)* [Online video]. December 11th 2014. Available from: https://www.youtube.com/watch?v=4mUII1HcsRg&ab_channel=KafkaWinstonWorld [Accessed 15th July 2015]

LawOfIdentity (2014) *"We Will Become Gods"* [Online video]. August 20th 2014. Available from: https://www.youtube.com/watch?v=5MmXHMaati0&ab_channel=LawOfIdentity [Accessed 23 July 2015]

Legal-dictionary (2015) *Habeas Corpus* [Online] Available from: http://legal-dictionary.thefreedictionary.com/habeas+corpus [Accessed 14th May 2015]

Mark Dice (2014) *Top Transhumanist Claims He Will Become God and Kill Anyone Who Tries to Stop Him!!!* [Online video] May 14th 2014. Available from: https://www.youtube.com/watch?v=KPJARo-5VXE&ab_channel=MarkDice [Accessed 24th July 2015]

Medical News Today (2015) *Paranoid Schizophrenia: Causes, Symptoms and Treatments* [Online] Available from: http://www.medicalnewstoday.com/articles/192621.php [Accessed 21st July 2015]

Megadeth (2001) *The World Needs a Hero* [CD] USA: Sanctuary Records Group Ltd

MK Ultra Compendium (1980) *Secret CIA Human Experiments in the United States: MK Ultra Mind Control Research Program.* [online video] May 26th 2012. Available from: https://www.youtube.com/watch?v=c4f9Hs0s1jQ&ab_channel=TheFilmArchives [Accessed: 22nd June 2015]

Mind-Computer (2012) *Synthetic telepathy "Artificial Telepathy"* [Online] Available from: http://mind-computer.com/2012/05/15/synthetic-telepathy-artificial-telepathy/ [Accessed 22nd June 2015]

Moss, S., (2009) *Evaluative conditioning* [online] Available from: http://www.psych-it.com.au/Psychlopedia/article.asp?id=312 [Accessed 28th June 2015]

Motherboard (2015) *Motherboard* [Online] Available from: http://motherboard.vice.com/en_uk [Accessed 28th July 2015]

MrCowShedder (2012) *Royal Babylon by Heathcote Williams (rough cut).* [Online video]. May 11th 2012. Available from: https://www.youtube.com/watch?v=jIukrdRhnpw&ab_channel=MrCowshedder [Accessed 14th July 2015]

MurdokDubstep (2010) *Where'd You Go – Fort Minor (Murdok Dubstep Remix)* [Online video]. July 22nd 2010. Available from: https://www.youtube.com/watch?v=7VdAvIf1Nc4&ab_channel=MurdokDubstep [Accessed 15th July 2015]

nature video (2013) *Reading minds* [Online video]. October 23rd 2013. Available from: https://www.youtube.com/watch?v=z8iEogscUl8&ab_channel=naturevideo [Accessed: 22nd July 2015]

New Scientist (2014) *Brain Decoder can eavesdrop on your inner voice* [Online] Available from: https://www.newscientist.com/article/mg22429934-000-brain-decoder-can-eavesdrop-on-your-inner-voice/ [Accessed 12th June 2015]

New Scientist (2015) *New Scientist* [Online] Available from: https://www.newscientist.com/ [Accessed 28th July 2015]

Non Mirage Truth Vision (2015) *CIA's Heart Attack Gun* [Online video]. Available from: https://www.youtube.com/watch?v=Uwy56QTV4cs&ab_channel=NonMirageTruthVision [Accessed 16th July 2015]

Paye, J-C., (2013) *The Suspension of Habeas Corpus in America* [Online] Available from: http://www.globalresearch.ca/the-suspension-of-habeas-corpus-in-america/5311701 [Accessed 20th May 2015]

Prigg, M., (2014) *Mindreading software could eavesdrop on your secret inner voice* [Online] Available from: *http://www.dailymail.co.uk/sciencetech/article-2814896/The-mindreading-machine-listen-voices-head-let-paralysed-speak-again.html* [Accessed 13th June 2015]

RainmanJhof (2011) *Boondox-Abadon* [Online video]. October 31st 2011. Available from: https://www.youtube.com/watch?v=C2bH4B5_83Q&ab_channel=RainmanJhof [Accessed 15th July]

Radar Online (2013) *Princess Dianna 'Killed By Bright Light Shone By Special Forces Soldiers Into Car She Was In'* [Online] Available from: http://radaronline.com/exclusives/2013/09/princess-diana-killed-died-death-forces-light-special-air-service/ [Accessed 17th July 2015]

Rense (2001) *Microchip Mind Control, Implants and Cybernetics* [Online] Available from: http://www.rense.com/general17/imp.htm [Accessed 20th June 2015]

Rense (2011) *Possible HAARP Locations Around the World* [Online] Available from: http://www.rense.com/general92/haarp.htm [Accessed 20th July 2015]

Russo, A., (1996) *Mad as Hell* [Online video]. May 10th 2011. Available from: https://www.youtube.com/watch?v=Zz4TI75MszQ&ab_channel=XRepublicTV [Accessed: 13th May 2015]

Russo, A., (2006) *Freedom to Fascism* [Online video]. May 10th 2011. Available from: https://www.youtube.com/watch?v=uNNeVu8wUak&ab_channel=RevolutionistsUnited [Accessed: 12th May 2015]

RT (2014) *Revolutionary way to 'switch off' pain discovered* [Online] Available from: http://www.rt.com/news/210031-revolutionary-painkiller-discovered-scientists/ [Accessed 19th July 2015]

RT (2015) *Living forever as a robot? Prototype lets humans upload their mind into mechanised 'heads'* [Online] Available from: http://www.rt.com/usa/229811-mind-clones-robot-afterlife/ [Accessed 27th June 2015]

SadSongs4You (2010) *Elton John –Candle In The Wind. With lyrics* [Online video]. August 23rd 2010. Available from: https://www.youtube.com/watch?v=80rHyABCb20&ab_channel=SadSongs4You [Accessed 17th July 2015]

Schechtman (2012) *The Story of my (Second) Life: Virtual Worlds and Narrative Identity,* Philosophy and Technology, Volume 25, Issue 3, pp. 329-343

Science Daily (2014) *'Off switch' for pain discovered: Activating the adenosine A3 receptor subtype is key to powerful pain relief* [Online] Available from: http://www.sciencedaily.com/releases/2014/11/141126132639.htm [Accessed 19th July 2015]

Sheen, M., Begich, N., & Robbins, W., (2005) *Holes in Heaven? H.A.A.R.P. & Advances in Tesla Technology* [Online video]. October 8th 2014. Available from: https://www.youtube.com/watch?v=SWVU6DKcjyA&ab_channel=documentary2014 [Accessed: 15th June 2015]

SimpleGirl4ewer (2007) *Britney Spears – Mona Lisa* [Online video]. March 18th 2007. Available from: https://www.youtube.com/watch?v=xEecXKUxl1s&ab_channel=SimpleGirl4ewer [Accessed 18th July 2015]

Star Wars Episode III: Revenge of the Sith (2005) Film. Directed by George Lucas. [DVD]. USA: 20 Century Fox

Stromberg, J., (2013) *Scientist Figure Out What You See While You're Dreaming* [Online] Available from: http://www.smithsonianmag.com/science-nature/scientists-figure-out-what-you-see-while-youre-dreaming-15553304/?no-ist [Accessed 22nd July 2015]

The 6th Day (2000) Film. Directed by Roger Spottiswoode. [DVD]. USA: Columbia Pictures

The Guardian (2015a) *The Guardian* [Online] Available from: http://www.theguardian.com/science [Accessed 28th July 2015]

The Guardian (2015b) *The Guardian* [Online] Available from: http://www.theguardian.com/uk/technology [Accessed 28th July 2015]

The Independent (2015a) The Independent [Online] Available from: http://www.independent.co.uk/news/science/ [Accessed 28th July 2015]

The Independent (2015b) The Independent [Online] Available from: http://www.independent.co.uk/life-style/gadgets-and-tech/ [Accessed 28th July 2015]

The Island (2005) Film. Directed by Michael Bay. [DVD]. USA: DreamWorks Pictures

The Manchurian Candidate (2004) Film. Directed by Jonathan Demme. [DVD]. USA: Paramount Pictures

TheNanoAge (2015) *Transhumanism and Posthumanism: The Future of Us (Humanity Plus)* [Online] Available from: *http://www.thenanoage.com/transhumanism-posthumanism.htm#transhuman* [Accessed: 30th May 2015]

Truthstream (2006) *Rigged USA Elections Exposed.* March 2nd 2006. Available from: https://www.youtube.com/watch?v=JEzY2tnwExs&ab_channel=truthstream [Accessed: 22th May 2015]

UC Berkeley Campus Life (2011) *Vision Reconstruction* [Online video]. December 11th 2011 Available from: https://www.youtube.com/watch?v=6FsH7RK1S2E&feature=youtu.be&ab_channel=UCBerkeleyCampusLife [Accessed 22nd July 2015]

Walcutt, D. L., (2013) *Stages of Sleep.* [Online] Available from: http://psychcentral.com/lib/stages-of-sleep/ [Accessed 5th June 2015]

Walther, E., Nagengast, B., & Trasselli, C., (2005). *Evaluative conditioning in social psychology: Facts and speculations.* Cognition and Emotion, 19, 175–196 In Moss, S., (2009) *Evaluative conditioning* [online] Available from: http://www.psych-it.com.au/Psychlopedia/article.asp?id=312 [Accessed 28th June 2015]

WhiteLiesVevo (2010) *White Lies – Bigger Than Us* [Online video]. November 18th 2010 Available from: https://www.youtube.com/watch?v=JW0yynlDmqQ&ab_channel=WhiteLiesVEVO [Accessed 18th July]

Winter, L., (2014) *Scientist Erase Memories with Light* [Online] Available from: http://www.iflscience.com/brain/scientists-erased-memories-light [Accessed 10th June 2015]

WorldTruth (2014) *The Georgia Guidestones* [Online] Available from: http://worldtruth.tv/the-georgia-guidestones-2/ [Accessed 16th May 2015]

YesEthan (2013) *Consciousness Science Kept Hidden* [Online Video] January 12th 2013. Available from: https://www.youtube.com/watch?v=LFSRTsLOiv0&ab_channel=YesEthan [Accessed 4th July 2015]

Legislation

Computer Misuse Act (1990) Section 3A, _Making, supplying or obtaining articles for use in offence under section 1 or 3_ [Online] Available from: http://www.legislation.gov.uk/ukpga/1990/18/section/3A [Accessed 8th May 2015]

Enterprise and Regulatory Reform Act (2013) Section 17, _Disclosures not protected unless believed to be made in the public interest._ [Online] Available from: http://www.legislation.gov.uk/ukpga/2013/24/section/17/enacted [Accessed 8th May 2015]

Public Interest Disclosure Act (1998) Section 43B, _Disclosures qualifying for protection._ [Online] Available from: http://www.legislation.gov.uk/ukpga/1998/23/section/1 [Accessed 8th May 2015]

Serious Crime Act (2015) Section 41 3ZA, _Unauthorised acts causing, or creating risk of, serious damage._ [Online] Available from: http://www.legislation.gov.uk/ukpga/2015/9/section/41/enacted [Accessed 8th May 2015]

Contact Information

Facebook

My Facebook is: https://www.facebook.com/donald.marshall.148
You can also press Ctrl+Click (hold "Ctrl" on your keyboard and left
"Click" with your mouse, on the image to your right).

I have a public wall on Facebook which starts from March 2012. In other words, all posts are
made public since March 2012 and you do not have to join my friends list or subscribe me to
see what I post (although you will have to have a Facebook account). I suggest that
newcomers start reading from March 2012, and be patient, and read everything. You can
read everything and learn the real truth of the world free of charge. I don't wish to write a
book, I am not looking to turn a profit from this; I want to crush these guys and shut down the
cloning centres!

Donald Marshall Forum

You can also view Proboards which has all my Facebook posts and have
been archived by Celine O'Carroll and Astral 7ight by visiting:

http://donaldmarshall.proboards.com/
You can also press Ctrl+Click (hold "Ctrl" on your keyboard and left
"Click" with your mouse, on the image to your right).

There is a search function on Proboards, and you can use this to search for and read all the
disclosures I have made regarding REM driven clones, the people involved and more. I
understand that it is human nature to want to know, which people have been to the cloning
centre as REM driven clones; therefore, use the search function to read about any public
figure which I have already covered that you have an inkling about. You can also post
anonymously on Proboards and Celine and other Administrators will transfer your question
onto Facebook which I'll answer.

Donald Marshall Revolution

Donald Marshall Revolution is a website which details a brief overview
of the Illuminati. http://donaldmarshallrevolution.com/
You can also press Ctrl+Click (hold "Ctrl" on your keyboard and left
"Click" with your mouse, on the image to your right).

Radio Presenters –Contact Donald Marshall

Anyone who sincerely wants to contact me for radio interviews on their show is welcome to do this. Please contact me through Proboards by leaving a message for me to contact you.

Professionals who understand "Consciousness Transfer" –Contact Donald Marshall

Any neuroscientists, engineers or professionals who understand how consciousness transfer works, and can provide me with a detailed methodology of how to block the consciousness transfer to my REM driven clone; please message me on Proboards, and this will be greatly appreciated.

Email

I currently do not have a contactable email address. In my original disclosure (Donald Marshall Proboards 2012), the email address has been compromised (hacked), and so has any other email accounts I created: Yahoo, hotmail, Gmail, AOL etc. It doesn't matter; they eventually get hacked; for whatever reason, the Illuminati do not want me to have an email account.

Made in the USA
Las Vegas, NV
19 January 2025